I0141127

AREA OF RESCUE

Laura Eason

BROADWAY PLAY PUBLISHING INC
New York
www.broadwayplaypublishing.com
info@broadwayplaypublishing.com

AREA OF RESCUE
© Copyright 2007 by Laura Eason

All rights reserved. This work is fully protected under the copyright laws of the United States of America. No part of this publication may be photocopied, reproduced, stored in a retrieval system, or transmitted, in any form or by any means, electronic, mechanical, recording, or otherwise, without the prior permission of the publisher. Additional copies of this play are available from the publisher.

For all other rights please contact the author at www.lauraeason.com.

Cover art compliments of Andhow! Theater Company

I S B N: 978-0-88145-345-4
First printing: June 2007

Book design: Marie Donovan
Word processing: Microsoft Word
Typographic controls: Ventura Publisher
Typeface: Palatino
Printed and bound in the U S A

The world premiere of AREA OF RESCUE opened on
9 June 2007, presented by Andhow! Theater Company
(Jessica Davis-Irons, Artistic Director; Andrew Irons,
Producing Director; Danya Haber, Associate Producer)
at the Connelly Theater in N Y C. The cast and creative
contributors were:

HEDY .... Kiki Hernandez
ALLEAH .... Abby Royle
MIA ....Jackie Chung
GORDON .... Arthur Aulisi
RUTH ING .... Hazel Medina
IDA HENRI ....Maria Cellario
IVO .... Omar Evans

Director ....Jessica Davis-Irons
Scenic design ....Neal Wilkinson
Lighting design ....Owen Hughes
Video design .... Dustin O'Neill
Costume design .... Becky Lasky
Sound & original composition .... Jill B C DuBoff
Production stage manager .... Kelly Anne Shaffer

CHARACTERS & SETTING

GORDON, *thirties, who recently lost his wife, Lily—restrained and soulful.*

RUTH ING, *fifties-sixties,* GORDON'*s mother in law, mother of Lily—grounded, the matriarch holding the family together.*

MIA, *twenty,* RUTH'*s daughter,* GORDON'*s sister-in-law, Lily's sister—conflicted over her simple view of the way the world.*

HEDY, *eleven,* GORDON *and Lily's daughter—still, thoughtful, very wise for her age.*

IVO, *twenty-three,* MIA'*s boyfriend, doing his service time—a seemingly sweet man who becomes the voice of authority.*

ALEEAH, *late twenties-early thirties, the housekeeper and nanny—in the last years of her citizenship program. She has put her opinions aside for years.*

IDA HENRI, *fifties-sixties, the* ING'*s next door neighbor.*

Casting note: It is important that the cast be of various racial/ethnic backgrounds—as a group and/or as individuals—so that no one racial/ethnic background is dominant.

Location: The action takes place in and around the ING *family home. Outside the front door there is a small field of birch trees.*

Time: The play takes place over the course of a few weeks in an imagined time in the near future.

To my parents for teaching me
the importance of questions
and to Jessica
for giving me the chance to ask them.

Scene 1

(A cloudy afternoon. Center stage is the living/kitchen area of a home, spare and uncluttered. Unobtrusively hanging near the front door are a couple of coats, a couple of hats and a couple of gas masks. A small powder room is off the living room. Stage left is a forest of birch trees that have been stripped of their leaves and branches.)

(HEDY, eleven, dressed in mourning with a hat, runs to the house. Around her neck is a laminated I D badge. She opens the front door and slams it behind her. She finds a remote control and presses some buttons.)

(On a wall, a film appears—an older man with a violin. He begins to narrate an early violin lesson. HEDY grabs her violin and plays along.

(ALEEAH appears at the door. She, too, is dressed in mourning with a hat and an I D badge [of a different color] around her neck. She enters and sees HEDY with the violin, takes the remote and pauses the film.)

ALEEAH: Hey, honey. I don't think we're going to do that today.

HEDY: It's Friday. I do my lesson on Friday.

ALEEAH: I think today is different.

HEDY: Why?

ALEEAH: *(Gently taking her violin)* You know. Because of your Mom. And because of you...

HEDY: I don't want anyone to do anything about that.

ALEEAH: We won't do anything you don't want us to.

HEDY: Not today.

ALEEAH: Whatever you want, honey.

HEDY: *(Re: the video)* Can I listen to the rest of the song?

ALEEAH: Sure, baby.

(ALEEAH turns the film back on. HEDY walks to the wall and leans against the image as the man plays. ALEEAH walks to the kitchen and puts on a kettle.)

(MIA, twnety, walks to the door. She is dressed in mourning with a hat and an I D badge. As she enters the house, she takes off her hat. She does not take off her I D badge. She goes to HEDY and hugs her. HEDY hugs her back. The image of the man plays over them. The sound of a beeping phone. MIA looks in her bag.)

MIA: *(To HEDY)* I'll be back in a sec, O K?

(She leaves the room. HEDY watches her until she's gone, then goes to the door and looks out the window next to it.)

(In the field of trees, GORDON, thirties, walks just ahead of RUTH, sixties. They are both dressed in mourning with hats and I D badges. As GORDON walks towards the house, he gets closer and closer to the ground until he falls. RUTH comforts him as he cries into his hands. HEDY watches all of this from the window.)

ALEEAH: Are you hungry, honey?

HEDY: My father fell down.

ALEEAH: Where?

HEDY: In the trees.

(ALEEAH turns off the film and looks out the window, seeing RUTH and GORDON. She quickly hustles HEDY away.)

ALEEAH: Why don't you have a little something to eat? I'll make you whatever you want. Name it.

HEDY: No, thanks. *(She goes back and leans against the now blank wall.)*

ALEEAH: You know, honey, if you want to have a lesson, I shouldn't stop you. I just thought of your father, maybe he'd want it quiet. But I know he'd want you to do whatever you want today, so—

HEDY: *(Plainly)* You don't have to be so nervous.

ALEEAH: *(After a moment)* I'm trying not to be.

(They look at each other for a moment. HEDY goes back to the window. GORDON comes with RUTH to the door. HEDY leaves the room.)

ALEEAH: Hedy?

(GORDON and RUTH come in and take off their hats and I D badges. GORDON sits on the couch.)

ALEEAH: I've put some water on.

RUTH: Thank you. Excuse me.

(RUTH goes to into the bathroom. As the scene outside continues, RUTH takes off her shirt. Standing in her slip, her chest is covered in small electrodes with wires attached from them to a small remote that is tucked into her waistband. She takes out the remote, looks at it, puts it back in her belt, sits and breathes.)

(MIA comes back out.)

MIA: Hedy's changing. Is that alright if people are coming over?

GORDON: *(A little too forcefully)* She can wear whatever she wants.

MIA: Okeydokey. *(Looking around)* Where's my Mom?

ALEEAH: In the rest-room.

MIA: She O K?

ALEEAH: She looks tired. But I think she's O K.

MIA: Ivo just called. He's coming over, said he'd like to pay his respects.

ALEEAH: *(To* GORDON*)* Do you want anything to eat, Mr. Gordon?

GORDON: No, thank you.

ALEEAH: Mia...?

MIA: No. Thanks.

ALEEAH: I'll put a little something together, just in case.

*(*ALEEAH *goes back to the kitchen.* MIA *sits on the couch at a distance from* GORDON*. A moment)*

MIA: She would have really liked it. Today.

*(*GORDON *nods.)*

MIA: It was nice of so many people to come.

*(*GORDON *nods.)*

GORDON: *(Re: snapping at her earlier)* I'm sorry.

MIA: It's alright.

GORDON: *(At a loss for words because of the larger circumstance)* I...uh...

*(*MIA *shakes her head in agreement, unable to get any words out.)*

(A knock at the door. It is MRS HENRI*. She has an I D badge around her neck and holds two large food containers.* MIA *looks out the window and heads towards the door.)*

MIA: It's Mrs Henri. I think she brought food.

GORDON: Tell her we're not up for seeing anyone.

MIA: Why? She's nice. She and Lily always got along...

GORDON: Please don't bring Lily into this.

MIA: She's looking in. She sees we're here.

GORDON: Tell her to leave the food and go away!

MIA: Gordon, you're being —

(RUTH *comes out of the bathroom, fully dressed and looking much more calm.* GORDON *and* MIA *catch themselves when they see her. Another knock on the door)*

RUTH: Is someone here?

MIA: Mrs Henri.

RUTH: Well, let her in. *(Calling)* Aleeah?

(ALEEAH *comes out and goes to the door. She lets* MRS HENRI *in.* RUTH *stands.)*

RUTH: It's kind of you to come by, Ida.

MRS HENRI: Please, Ruth, sit. All of you. I don't want to tax you. I just wanted to drop off a few things that I hope will make today a little easier.

MIA: That's so nice.

RUTH: Thank you.

(MRS HENRI *walks the containers to the kitchen area and* ALEEAH *takes charge of them.)*

MRS HENRI: *(To* ALEEAH*)* There is a hot dish for dinner, which, if you want to put it in the oven, Leigh, at a low temperature, it'll be fine for quite a while. You can just cut little pieces for individual servings as people want them, you needn't serve everyone at once.

ALEEAH: *(Nodding and forcing a smile)* Great.

MRS HENRI: *(To* RUTH*)* And, I hope you don't mind, I did take the liberty, and I hope I made the right choice in this regard, I brought a cake for Hedy. I know it is not a day to celebrate, but I thought maybe it would cheer her up a little. I didn't put any candles or anything, but I thought even the gesture might cheer her a little bit.

GORDON: Hedy is eleven years old today. We will celebrate that. We will and we do. Thank you, Mrs Henri. Thank you for stopping by.

RUTH: And for your thoughtfulness.

MRS HENRI: Is she in her room? Little Hedy?

MIA: She's changing.

MRS HENRI: Well, I made her that velvet cake with buttercream frosting that she always seems to like, so I hope that will do for her.

RUTH: It'll more than do, thank you.

MIA: You've always been so thoughtful, Mrs Henri. I know it would have meant a lot to Lily.

(HEDY *comes out. Seeing* MRS HENRI *she stops in her tracks.*)

MRS HENRI: Hello, Hedy.

HEDY: Hello.

MRS HENRI: I was just telling your Grandmother that I brought a velvet cake in honor of your special day today. Did you know it's your golden birthday, dear?

HEDY: No.

MRS HENRI: Do you know what that is?

HEDY: No.

MRS HENRI: It's when the day of your birthday and the year you are turning are the same. Today you are eleven and it's the eleventh, so this is your golden birthday.

HEDY: I don't think we're celebrating.

MRS HENRI: I know we all are very sad today.

GORDON: Yes, we are.

MRS HENRI: But, there is comfort today, too.

(As MRS HENRI *talks,* HEDY *slowly smashes herself flat against the back wall.)*

MRS HENRI: A day like today brings terrible sadness for us, for the one *we* have lost, but it also brings joy— joy in knowing that Lily has moved ahead... *(She performs a ritualistic gesture, moving her hand from her mouth to her heart with an open, flat hand. With the gesture:)* "As it has been told".

*(*MIA *and* RUTH *both mimic the gesture completely as* RUTH *repeats the phrase. Gordon does the gesture as well, but less fully.)*

RUTH: As it has been told.

HEDY: *(To* RUTH*)* May I go out, Meme? Just to walk a little in the trees. I won't go far.

RUTH: Put your hat on. And some lotion.

*(*ALEEAH *hands* HEDY *a bottle of white lotion.* HEDY *starts to put it on her face and hands as she goes to the door.)*

RUTH: Hedy, thank Mrs Henri before you go.

HEDY: *(Quickly)* Thank you.

*(*HEDY *crosses to* GORDON. *She hugs him suddenly, very forcefully.* GORDON *takes her face in his hands.)*

GORDON: We'll have some cake for your birthday. O K?

*(*HEDY *nods and goes out the door. Outside, she wanders around in the trees.)*

MRS HENRI: How is she holding up, poor dear?

RUTH: She will be fine.

(A long beat. GORDON *gets up and walks to the window watching* HEDY.*)*

ALEEAH: Would you like something, Mrs Henri?

MRS HENRI: No, dear, thank you, I don't want to be any trouble.

(*The kettle whistles.*)

MRS HENRI: Oh, are you making tea?

ALEEAH: I'll bring it out in a minute.

MRS HENRI: I don't want to trouble you all—

ALEEAH: It's no trouble. It's for everyone.

MRS HENRI: Well, tea sounds very pleasant, very pleasant indeed.

(MIA *looks at her phone and punches at the keypad.*)

MIA: Will you excuse me just a minute, please?

MRS HENRI: Of course, my dear.

RUTH: Please, sit, make yourself comfortable, Ida.

MRS HENRI: (*Sitting*) Mrs Gibson and I were both remarking on how beautiful the flowers were.

RUTH: I'm pleased you thought so.

MRS HENRI: She came over for a bit after the service and we both were so struck by how lovely they were.

RUTH: They were lovely.

MRS HENRI: We got home some time ago. You must of had a bit of nice quiet time alone with the family.

RUTH: Yes, we did.

MRS HENRI: I'm sorry your boys weren't able to make it home.

RUTH: Yes.

MRS HENRI: But the work they are doing is very important for us all.

RUTH: Yes, of course. *(After a moment)* How is your hip coming along?

MRS HENRI: Almost as good as new. It's amazing what they can do these days.

RUTH: Yes, it is.

MRS HENRI: And you?

RUTH: Still struggling along.

MRS HENRI: *(Quietly to* RUTH*)* Now, Ruth, you mustn't despair. I remember when I lost my Josephine. I never thought I'd be able to feel happiness again. But, you know, as I do, that this loss is only temporary, the greater plan is at work here—

RUTH: Of course.

MRS HENRI: With every sadness is a companion joy! *(As though quoting)* As it has been told.

RUTH: *(Quietly in the same cadence)* As it has been told.

MRS HENRI: And the double joy of Hedy's birthday falling today—and not just her birthday but her golden birthday!

*(*ALEEAH *brings out a tray with tea and some small tea cakes.)*

ALEEAH: *(Re: the tea)* It should steep another minute in the pot.

RUTH: Thank you, Aleeah.

MRS HENRI: Thank you, dear.

*(*ALEEAH *goes back into the kitchen.)*

MRS HENRI: *(Quietly to* RUTH*)* Is this her last year?

RUTH: She was placed with us just after Hedy was born. So, yes, that's eleven. It's gone so fast.

MRS HENRI: Will you keep her on? For Hedy's sake?

RUTH: We would like to, but it's Aleeah's choice now.

MRS HENRI: Of course. I can't imagine her not wanting to stay. *(After a moment)* But a lot of these people don't realize how good the system is until they try and work outside of it. She hasn't any family placed here, does she?

RUTH: No. They didn't make it out in time.

MRS HENRI: Pity. *(After a moment, quietly)* But... one should be a little careful, Ruth. Mrs Gibson had a terrible time with one of her placements who stayed on. You know, once they're no longer government monitored, they can advocate for any crazy idea they might believe! *(She shakes her head, then looks to the teapot.)* Well, that must be about ready.

(MRS HENRI pours the tea. She gives a cup to RUTH.)

RUTH: Thank you.

(She pours another.)

MRS HENRI: Gordon?

GORDON: *(Looking to her)* Yes?

MRS HENRI: Tea?

GORDON: *(Back to the window)* No, thank you.

(MIA comes back into the room.)

MRS HENRI: *(To MIA)* Tea, dear?

MIA: Uh, sure. Thanks. *(She sits down next to RUTH.)* So, Mrs Henri, we saw they finally reached your planting beds.

MRS HENRI: Oh, yes. I must admit, I was sad to see them go.

RUTH: You had made such a beautiful spot.

MRS HENRI: Well, yes. But what are flowers in comparison to our safety?

MIA: Of course.

MRS HENRI: They weren't sure when they made the plan if they'd need all our land out back. But, it turns out they did, so, there they went.

GORDON: Hedy will never get over it.

MRS HENRI: The flower beds?

GORDON: No, the trees. She'll never get over the trees. It was bad enough when the birds left.

MIA: *(Remembering something)* Oh. *(She gets up and gets a small white, wrapped box out of a cabinet.)*

RUTH: She was very attached to the birds. She always wanted to have one.

MIA: That's only because you told her people used to have birds as pets. But look— *(She opens the box.)* It's for Hedy. It's from Lily. She had me hide it. Should I give it to her or should we wait...?

GORDON: We'll ask her.

MRS HENRI: Shoot! I meant to bring over this beautifully illustrated "transition" we have. *(To MIA, explaining)* When my husband moved ahead, we shared with the grandchildren and I think it helped them quite a bit.

GORDON: Excuse me. *(He abruptly leaves the window and crosses to the bathroom.)*

MIA: I'm sure Hedy would love it.

MRS HENRI: One comfort you must have was how strongly Lily believed—she was "a face of the faith".

RUTH: Yes.

(The women sip their tea.)

(In the bathroom, GORDON projects a ten second video clip of a beautiful women standing on a ferry boat. She looks off, unaware that her image is being capture. The clip cycles through a few times, as GORDON puts his head in his hands.)

(Out in the trees, HEDY wanders. She is approached by IVO, who is dressed in a uniform.)

IVO: Hey Hedder.

HEDY: Hi.

IVO: How're you doing?

HEDY: Fine.

(HEDY sits on the ground, looking at the trees. IVO joins her. They sit looking up.)

IVO: You can see so much sky.

HEDY: It's cloudy.

IVO: Yeah, I know it's cloudy. I just mean since they stripped the trees. You couldn't see an inch of sky before.

(Suddenly, a huge wind burst fills the stage—it is loud and violent. IVO covers HEDY to protect her from it.)

(In the living room, the women, hearing the wind, move to the window to look out, checking on HEDY.)

(Then, just as suddenly, the wind stops. IVO casually waves at the women in the window. They nod and sit back down with their tea. IVO and HEDY straighten themselves up a bit.)

IVO: Not such a bad one.

HEDY: No. *(After a moment)* Was it just for the birds?

IVO: What?

HEDY: Did they strip the trees to make the birds go away?

IVO: No. Those birds were O K. They're taking down the trees to clear this whole patch here. Didn't you see how they cleared the neighbor's yards?

HEDY: Yes.

IVO: Well, they're clearing all of it.

HEDY: Why?

IVO: Didn't your father tell you?

HEDY: No.

IVO: Well, he should've because your family is one of the lucky ones.

HEDY: Why?

IVO: They're making an Area of Rescue here.

HEDY: What's that?

IVO: An Area of Rescue? You never heard of one?

HEDY: Nope.

IVO: Your father never told you about it?

HEDY: *(Covering)* Um, maybe he did. But I don't remember.

IVO: Well, it's a lucky thing to have right outside your door, I'll tell you! You see, if something happens, you know, something...unforeseen...and you hear the siren go —

HEDY: Like when they test it on Tuesday mornings?

IVO: Right. But this is for when it's not a test.

HEDY: When's that?

IVO: When something happens. Something that'd mean you'd have to leave home for a while.

HEDY: Like a flood or a volcano? I saw that city last month that had that volcano and everyone had to leave.

IVO: Well, yeah. But we don't have to worry about volcanoes around here so much.

HEDY: So, like one of the bad storms?

IVO: Yeah.

HEDY: Or an explosion?

IVO: Yeah, that, too.

HEDY: My Uncles, they know about explosions.

IVO: I know they do.

HEDY: They're far away so they couldn't come home for Mom's funeral.

IVO: I know. I'm sure you're sad about that, but they're doing really important work.

HEDY: That's what Aunt Mia says.

IVO: Aunt Mia is right. They're helping keep people safe. And that's what the Area of Rescue is going to do—keep you safe!

HEDY: How?

IVO: Well, when the sirens go off, everyone is going to know to come to their closest area. Now, all this will be gone and there'll be a flat slab. In the center, there'll be a door. And that door will go very far, deep into the ground. And everyone will gather here and you'll either get picked up and taken somewhere safe, or you'll go down in the ground and be safe there. It's so people who're trying to take care of you will know just where you are and don't have to go looking all around. Everyone will know to come here.

HEDY: But won't the bad guys know, too?

IVO: How do you mean?

HEDY: Won't the bad guys know about these? We'll all be in one place, like sitting ducks.

IVO: Well, there's going to be a lot of them. Millions of them. We're making them for almost every neighborhood. So, there'll be too many for the bad guys to get.

HEDY: Oh.

IVO: And you're lucky enough to have it right outside your door!

HEDY: But my Mom said the... *(Finding the word)* Pendulum...?

IVO: *(Confirming her pronunciation)* Yeah, pendulum.

HEDY: That we were O K—the pendulum was swinging—and nothing really bad has happened here...

IVO: Yeah, but, the thing about a pendulum, Hedy, is that it always swings back.

HEDY: *(Slowly, thinking about this)* Right. And back.

IVO: And back again.

HEDY: *(Realizing)* Until it stops. *(After a long moment)* Did you ever see the blue bird?

IVO: *(Not having heard her)* What's that?

HEDY: There was a blue bird. Just one. The rest were black. But there was one blue one. I wondered how that blue one got here, where he came from.

IVO: No, I never saw a blue one. Just the regular old black ones. I saw a red one once at the zoo.

HEDY: How will they do it?

IVO: Do what?

HEDY: Get rid of the trees?

IVO: Cut them down. Then, burn up what's left.

(They look at the trees for a moment.)

HEDY: I liked that blue one.

IVO: Mia said you were awful sad to see the birds go. But, once you get a little older, you'll see. This is much more important. It's important for everyone. For your future. For everyone's future.

(HEDY *points to* IVO's *I D badge.*)

HEDY: Why is yours green?

IVO: It's green because I'm doing my service time. And it's got that border around it to show I'm in my second year.

HEDY: Is Aleeah's orange because she's from another country?

IVO: Aleeah's is different—bigger and such—because she's in the last phase of her citizenship program.

HEDY: But why is her's *orange*?

IVO: Well, her's is orange because of her faith—she has a different one than most of us that live here.

HEDY: *(Surprised)* But that's O K.

IVO: Oh, of course it's O K. It's absolutely O K. Everyone is free to believe whatever they want! But, it's a really important thing to people, so we like to keep track, because it's so important. It's something to take note of. *(Holding out his I D badge)* So, we note it here—name, address, height, weight, faith, birthday...

HEDY: Oh.

IVO: And speaking of birthdays. *(He pulls out a little bundle of tissue paper.)*

HEDY: What is it?

IVO: It's a present. It's a surprise. For your birthday.

HEDY: Can I open it later?

IVO: Uh, sure. Whenever you want.

HEDY: Thanks.

IVO: Well, I'd better go in. *(After walking a few steps)* I'm real sorry about your Mom, Hedy.

HEDY: Thanks.

IVO: And if the fault lies with anyone who ran the ferryboat, well, your family will be compensated. You should know that.

HEDY: O K.

IVO: See you in there in a minute.

HEDY: O K.

(Ivo knocks on the door. MIA gets up to get it.)

MIA: *(Happily)* There he is.

MRS HENRI: *(Quietly to RUTH)* That's a good boy. He's done very well in his service years.

(IVO and MIA join RUTH and MRS HENRI.)

IVO: *(Nodding in greeting)* Mrs Ing. Mrs Henri. *(To RUTH)* It was a lovely service, Mrs Ing.

RUTH: Thank you, Ivo.

IVO: Again, I'm sorry for your loss.

RUTH: Thank you. I know you've been a comfort to Mia.

IVO: You know, I lost my brother about five years ago. Loss in combat is hard, but at least you know *why*? An accident is hard that way, different. But, I understand how she feels.

RUTH: Well, I know you've been a comfort.

(IVO pulls out a small flat package.)

IVO: I was asked by my supervisor to bring this with me. It's from Dean and Rohm. They sent it last night.

RUTH: Thank you. I wasn't sure they'd be able to send anything. We'll watch it a little later.

(GORDON *emerges from the bathroom.*)

IVO: *(Nodding hello)* Gordon.

GORDON: *(Nodding back)* Ivo.

IVO: I brought something that Dean and Rohm sent, a message for the family. I've given it to Ruth.

GORDON: Thank you.

RUTH: *(To* IVO) It will mean a lot to everyone. Especially Hedy.

IVO: I'm sure they were sad not to be here. But, they're doing important work.

MRS HENRI: Yes.

MIA: Yes.

RUTH: Yes.

ALEEAH: Can I get you some tea, Mister Ivo?

IVO: I'm fine, thanks.

ALEEAH: Something cold to drink?

IVO: Well, if it's no trouble. I'd take a soda or something if you have it.

(ALEEAH *goes to get him something.*)

IVO: I've come, of course, as Mia's friend, as a friend of all of you, but I've also come in an official capacity.

MRS HENRI: *(After a moment)* Well, I'll go. I don't want to be in the way.

RUTH: You're welcome to stay. I'm sure there's nothing confidential, is there, Ivo?

IVO: No, Ma'am. Just letting you know that there will be a full investigation of the accident. And if there's any liability on behalf of the ferry drivers, you'll be compensated, I guarantee you that.

RUTH: It was a terrible accident, but we don't need to place any blame.

IVO: They should've known better then to set off in waves like that. You should be compensated for your loss if they bear any responsibility.

GORDON: There is no compensation for our loss.

IVO: Of course. But money can help. I know Aleeah is eligible for salary soon. It could help you keep her on, which I'm sure Hedy would like. I know they're close.

(ALEEAH *brings the soda over to* IVO.)

RUTH: Please tell your superiors that we appreciate it, but we don't require an investigation.

IVO: I'm afraid it *is* required. Anytime there's an unusual death, we have to investigate.

GORDON: It was an accident. It wasn't unusual.

IVO: *(To the whole room)* In a few days, we'll talk more, get a fuller account of what happened, everyone's point of view.

RUTH: Of course, whatever we can do.

MIA: If those ferrymen knew the weather was unsafe, they should pay.

RUTH: Mia! We do not believe in vengeance.

MIA: I'm not speaking of vengeance. I'm speaking of what's right!

RUTH: Perhaps we should have some cake.

(RUTH *nods to* ALEEAH *who goes to the door and calls* HEDY *in.)*

ALEEAH: Hedy!

RUTH: *(To* IVO*)* Mrs Henri was kind enough to make a cake for Hedy. I don't think we'll sing...

MRS HENRI: But a little cake will do us good!

*(*MRS HENRI *goes to the kitchen.* ALEEAH *enters just in time to see her.* HEDY *goes and leans against the back wall.)*

ALEEAH: I can cut it, Mrs Henri.

MRS HENRI: This cake is a bit moister than what you're used to, I think. So, I'll do the cutting honors if you can get me some plates.

IVO: *(To* GORDON*)* I was telling Hedy about the progress on the rescue area.

GORDON: *(Attempting good humor)* I didn't think they were really going to go through with all of that.

IVO: Yeah, well, people wanted them.

GORDON: Did they, really?

IVO: *(Nodding)* Some people had to give up their land and some people lost their homes, but we've had almost no complaints and only a couple law suits... considering the scale of the project, that's quite something...

GORDON: Huh.

IVO: And the number of jobs its created has been pretty amazing.

MRS HENRI: Well, my planting beds were casualties just last week.

IVO: That's too bad. But all for the common good, I suppose.

MRS HENRI: Oh, I'm not complaining. I put a few things in barrels and had Carr and Micah haul them up to my roof— *(Explaining to* IVO*)* Those are my son Edward's boys. *(Back to the group)* I saved quite a few things. Only I'll be able to enjoy them, but I did save them.

IVO: That was industrious of you.

MRS HENRI: The instructions were in the last month's bulletin. Very informative.

IVO: I'm glad.

GORDON: How long before the trees...?

IVO: A couple of weeks at the most. Maybe sooner.

HEDY: They're going to burn them up.

MRS HENRI: *(To ALEEAH)* Have you any white plates, my dear? This cake doesn't show itself off well on dark plates. White plates are the thing. That's what professional chefs use, you know. Plain, stark white— to show off the food.

RUTH: How much more time in service for you, Ivo?

IVO: Six more months of required time

MRS HENRI: *(Looking at some plates)* Oh, yes, those will do very nicely.

IVO: But I'm thinking of staying in. Everything that's profitable is connected to service, you know? Security, energy, waste. It's all tied up. And it's a good living, enough to support a large family.

RUTH: Your family is what? Seven, I thought?

IVO: Yes, seven. Although, we lost my brother, as you know. And there was a little girl, just after me, but she didn't make it.

(ALEEAH and MRS HENRI bring the cake to the table. They all take a plate of cake and a fork.)

MRS HENRI: Here we are!

RUTH: It looks delicious, Ida. Thank you.

MRS HENRI: Well, I hope it tastes as good as it looks!

GORDON: Do you want a piece of cake, Hedy? It's for you.

(HEDY *comes over and sits on* GORDON's *lap, tucking her head between his head and his shoulder.)*

GORDON: You want to share mine?

(HEDY *nods.)*

MRS HENRI: Well, happy golden birthday, Hedy!

IVO: Happy birthday!

MIA: Happy birthday.

(RUTH *takes* HEDY's *hand and kisses it. They eat for a moment in silence.)*

RUTH: This is delicious.

IVO: I'll say!

MRS HENRI: Well, thank you. What do you think Hedy?

(HEDY *takes a small bite without looking up.)*

RUTH: You must give us the recipe. I'm sure Aleeah would be happy to have it.

MRS HENRI: Well, it is a family secret. *(Giggling alone)* But, maybe just this once!

MIA: I have a present. Do you want to open a present, Hedy?

GORDON: *(To* HEDY*)* It's up to you, honey. We'd be happy for you to open a present. Or if you'd rather wait, we can do that, too.

(HEDY *nods.* MIA *produces a flat dress box.* HEDY *opens it finding a really pretty dress inside.)*

MIA: Do you recognize it?

(HEDY *nods vigorously.)*

MIA: I had it altered for you. I was going to get you something new, but I know how much you loved this one.

HEDY: Thank you.

(HEDY hugs MIA. IVO takes out the tissue paper wrapped object and puts it on the table.)

IVO: Who's that from?

MIA: Oh, Ivo, you shouldn't have!

IVO: Happy to. Go on, Hedy.

(HEDY unwraps it. It is a small pin.)

IVO: You know what that is?

HEDY: No.

IVO: *(Pointing to the pin)* See that, that insignia means bravery. This is the real pin they give you to honor you for exceptional bravery.

MRS HENRI: How about that! That is one of the most special things I've ever seen.

IVO: I got permission from my supervisor. He said it'd be alright, considering the circumstances and all.

MIA: *(Kissing his cheek)* That was very thoughtful of you.

(HEDY points to the white box on the table.)

HEDY: What's that?

MIA: That's from your Mom.

HEDY: *(After a moment)* How?

MIA: She bought it a couple of weeks ago.

RUTH: Mia knew where she hid it.

HEDY: Oh.

GORDON: You don't have to open it. You can save it if you want.

(HEDY *goes to the box and opens it slowly. When she sees what's inside, she drops it in fright and runs to* ALEEAH.)

ALEEAH: It's O K, baby.

GORDON: *(Picking up the box)* What's wrong, honey?

HEDY: It's dead. It was in the box too long. It's dead.

MIA: *(Taking the box)* No, it's a toy, honey, it's not real. See? Look.

(MIA *takes a lifelike looking bluebird out of the box. She turns a switch and it chirps.* HEDY *goes and looks at it.*)

MIA: She knew how sad you were about the bluebird. And she knew you always wanted a little bird of your own.

(HEDY *takes the bird in her hand. It chirps. All eyes are on the bird.*)

(Transition)

(Perhaps it snows orange snow or there is a solar eclipse)

Scene 2

(HEDY *is out wandering with her bird in the trees.* ALEEAH *sits near her.* GORDON *and* RUTH *talk hotly in the living room.*)

GORDON: He knows by now. Of course, he does. They examined her body. Anyone would have seen.

RUTH: You need to be calm.

GORDON: How can I explain Lily and I being on *that* ferry?

RUTH: The hospital. Tie it somehow to the hospital.

GORDON: Yes, but—

(MIA *comes into the room.*)

RUTH: *(Covering)* But she and Aleeah are so close. Don't you think it's important we maintain their relationship?

GORDON: Let's ask, Mia.

MIA: What?

RUTH: It seems Aleeah is thinking of not staying on. How hard should we try to convince her?

MIA: *(Quietly after checking that* ALEEAH *is outside)*
I don't mean anything bad by this, Gordon, but
Lily wanted Hedy taught in school—not at home—
because she wanted her to get a certain *moral* education.
She didn't think she would get that here with Aleeah—
who she loved, but... you know. So, I think we should
let her go.

GORDON: Alright. Thanks.

*(*IVO *arrives with* MRS HENRI *in the forest.* MRS HENRI *and*
IVO *stop for a moment and talk with* HEDY *and* ALEEAH.
MIA *sees them out the window.)*

MIA: Mrs. Henri's going to take Hedy for something to eat.

RUTH: Aleeah can take her.

MIA: Ivo wants to talk to Aleeah, too.

*(*MRS HENRI *walks off with a reluctant* HEDY. IVO *and*
ALEEAH *go to the door.* MIA *opens it and they all cross
back into the living-room.)*

IVO: Good afternoon everyone.

RUTH: Good afternoon, Ivo. We just finished lunch.
Would you like a sandwich or something?

IVO: Thank you, no. Please, everyone, sit. I want this to
be as comfortable as possible.

RUTH: We know you have our best interest in mind.

IVO: So, as I said, we want to go over what happened. An unusual accident like that, it's important we get the facts.

(RUTH, GORDON *and* ALEEAH *sit on the couch as* IVO *stands at a distance from them.* MIA *sits near where* IVO *stands.*)

IVO: Gordon, I'd like to start with you, if I may.

GORDON: Of course.

IVO: Can you tell me about the accident from your point of view?

GORDON: *(After a moment)* We were on the ferry and the weather was bad. Lily was standing out on the deck. I tried to get her to go in, but you know how she is, very stubborn. I was holding her arm, which was wet and slippery from the spray. The boat lurched suddenly and she slipped over. I tried to hold her hand with my hand, but I couldn't. I knew that the water was very dangerous so I threw in the life ring, so I'd have something to hold onto in the water and dove in. But I couldn't find her. She had that heavy coat on—

RUTH: The swing coat.

GORDON: It must have been so heavy in the water. It was only a few seconds, even though it felt like forever. I must have been yelling because one of the crew men was on the deck right after I jumped in. The storm passed quickly and we looked and looked but we couldn't find her.

IVO: And they found her body the next day.

GORDON: Yes.

IVO: I read the report from the doctor that examined her.

GORDON: Yes?

IVO: Did you know she was pregnant?

GORDON: Yes, yes I did.

IVO: But you hadn't made it public knowledge?

GORDON: No. *(After a moment)* We've had a lot of problems over the years. We just wanted to wait to make sure everything was going to be alright.

IVO: And was it alright?

GORDON: Um, no. It wasn't.

IVO: Had you been to see Doctor Edvan last week?

GORDON: Yes.

IVO: Well, when we spoke with him—

GORDON: You spoke to him?

IVO: Yes. He told me something. Do you know what he might have told me?

GORDON: I assume he told you that our baby had died.

IVO: Yes, he did. And I'm sorry about that.

GORDON: Thank you.

IVO: And so was he.

GORDON: Yes. He was very compassionate.

IVO: He said she was five months along?

GORDON: Yes, five months.

IVO: So, what was the procedure?

GORDON: He didn't tell you?

IVO: I'd like for you to tell me what you understood it to be.

GORDON: They did a bunch of tests to make sure Lily was alright and then we made a birth appointment. *(Explaining)* They induce and the pregnancy is concluded that way.

IVO: I imagine that would be very difficult.

GORDON: Yes, well...

IVO: So, you scheduled an appointment?

GORDON: Yes. We saw Doctor Edvan on a Tuesday and the next birth appointment he had was the following Wednesday.

IVO: Over a week?

GORDON: He's very busy, as I'm sure you know.

IVO: That must have been difficult.

GORDON: We spent a lot of time in 'rumination and reflection'.

IVO: I'm sure you did.

GORDON: It always helped Lily.

IVO: But not you?

GORDON: Honestly, no. Not as much.

IVO: So, Friday came.

GORDON: Yes. Friday.

IVO: And what happened?

GORDON: Well, the night before Lily was talking, the doctor probably told you about the test?

IVO: Yes.

GORDON: So, you know that even if the child had lived, it would have had some significant problems.

IVO: Physical and mental problems.

GORDON: Yes. Both. Significant.

IVO: But still a "face of the faith" —as valued as any.

RUTH: Of course.

IVO: As it has been told.

(IVO *performs the ritualistic gesture, moving his hand from his mouth to his heart with an open, flat hand.* MIA *and* RUTH *both mimic the gesture completely.* GORDON *does the gesture as well, but less fully.* ALEEAH *does not do the gesture.*)

IVO: So, you and Lily were talking...?

GORDON: We were talking. And, as you know, across the water, there is the Children's Hospital, for children with difficulties. She said she wanted to go and visit them. I have no other explanation. She just wanted to see the children there.

IVO: Do you know why?

GORDON: Most of those children have been left in the care of the state. I think that maybe she imagined bringing one of them home.

IVO: Really?

GORDON: I don't know for sure, she didn't say that. But...she was so happy to have another child—and was ready for whatever that child was going to be.

IVO: Why didn't you ever adopt?

GORDON: What?

IVO: You only have Hedy. Just one.

GORDON: We had many problems.

IVO: And you didn't want to adopt?

GORDON: It's not that we didn't want to... Lily just wanted to have our own. I don't know.

IVO: So, you got on the ferry to go to the Children's Hospital. At what time?

GORDON: It was 10 AM.

IVO: Were there a lot of passengers on the ferry?

GORDON: Hardly any.

IVO: Not a busy time.

GORDON: No.

IVO: And how was Lily?

GORDON: How was she?

IVO: What was her state of mind?

GORDON: She was alright. I mean she was upset about the baby, but she was alright.

IVO: The Captain said she seemed nervous.

GORDON: Oh?

IVO: He said she was nervous. And that it reminded him of other women he sees on the ferry, who usually ride at the quiet time of day.

GORDON: *(Getting upset)* What are you—

RUTH: Ivo, if you've something to ask, you should just come out and ask it.

IVO: Have you heard of Doctor Emma Uda?

GORDON: Hasn't everyone?

IVO: So, you know what she does?

GORDON: Yes.

IVO: Were you going to see Doctor Uda?

GORDON: Our baby was already dead. What would I need to see Doctor Uda for?

IVO: So, no?

GORDON: No.

IVO: Did you speak with the Captain about the weather?

GORDON: Yes, I did.

IVO: What was that conversation?

GORDON: I expressed concern about the weather. I said we were fine either way—that we wouldn't blame him if it was too rough to travel.

IVO: He said you were very insistent on going. He said you offered him money to help him make his decision.

GORDON: There was another couple on the boat. It must have been that man.

IVO: He said it was the man who's wife fell in the water—that you offered him extra money to cross in the bad weather.

GORDON: Well, it wasn't me. I didn't offer him anything.

IVO: Why did you take the clip?

GORDON: Which clip?

IVO: The clip on the ferry? As it pulled away we have a record of you taking a ten second clip of Lily looking out at the water.

GORDON: *(Shaky)* Oh...

IVO: Why did you take that clip? It doesn't seem like this was a point in time you'd want to remember, add to the family reel...

GORDON: I... I don't know. It was an impulse. I can't explain it. *(With difficulty)* She just looked really... her hair in that light...I...?

IVO: *(Seeing GORDON's difficulty)* Alright. Thank you.

(GORDON gets up and goes to the window, looking out.)

IVO: Aleeah, how did she seem to you?

ALEEAH: Mrs Lily?

IVO: Yes.

ALEEAH: She was very happy about the baby.

IVO: How was she just before the accident?

ALEEAH: She was upset. She would cry. But she would, as you say, "ruminate and reflect" and then feel better. She said she knows it is part of your "greater plan".

IVO: I see.

ALEEAH: But she said it was strange, too.

IVO: What was?

ALEEAH: That the baby was still with her, in her body, but moved ahead, too.

IVO: Well, it's the spirit that matters, not the body.

ALEEAH: She was afraid because the baby was so little, not a full person yet and it would be scared and alone.

IVO: The spirit has no age. It is know from the first moment, it wouldn't be alone.

ALEEAH: I know that is your custom.

IVO: But not yours?

ALEEAH: No. For us, someone you knew in your life becomes your guide in the next. When her father, Mister Ing, passed on some years ago, I told her this. And it seemed to bring her comfort. But with this baby, she got afraid. She knew that the only person the baby knows is *her*. And she worried for him being alone.

IVO: Lily was worried?

ALEEAH: She said she wished she could put the baby in her father's arms, introduce them, so that he could take care of the little one.

IVO: She *said* this?

RUTH: Aleeah, you know Lily loved and respected you, but she did not think that. She wasn't worried about the baby, not like that.

IVO: Yes, Lily knew better than most what is told about the transition and moving ahead—the teachings are clear.

ALEEAH: How can they be clear? No one's ever been there—not even the teachers.

RUTH: *(Quietly)* Aleeah.

IVO: *(Smiling good-naturedly)* I can see who gets "freedom of conversation and conversion" in a couple of months, can't I?

ALEEAH: I'm sorry. I got carried away.

IVO: No, it's the passion of faith. Even though you aren't "on our team", so to speak, faith respects faith.

ALEEAH: Thank you, Mister Ivo. *(She goes to the kitchen.)*

IVO: Mia? *(A little more gentle with her)* Can you tell me about the last time you saw Lily?

MIA: It was that morning. Friday morning.

IVO: What did she say to you?

MIA: I found out about the baby the night before, what had happened. We talked through some things.

IVO: Can you tell me what they were...?

(MIA glances to GORDON.)

IVO: Can you all give us a minute?

RUTH: Of course.

(GORDON nods and steps out into the trees. RUTH stands and begins to go.

MIA: Mom, can you stay?

(RUTH nods and sits next to her.)

MIA: You know what Lily was like. Very understanding. Very forgiving. We talked about the

baby and how Gordon was doing and I told her I was
worried.

IVO: You were worried about Gordon?

MIA: Yes. *(After a breath)* He's a good man. When Dad
died, he really stepped in, didn't he, Mom?

(Off RUTH'*s nod)*

MIA: And Lily really loved him. But... *(After a moment)*
You know how he is now. He doesn't believe in
anything anymore. He didn't use to be like that.
You remember, Mom.

(Off Ruth's nod)

MIA: I just wanted to tell her I was worried about the
way Gordon was talking to Hedy. I don't want her
to be afraid, to have to live her life afraid.

IVO: Afraid of what?

MIA: Of everything, you know? *(Explaining)* I heard
Gordon talking to Hedy about the baby. She was asking
all these really important questions and all he could
say was, "I don't know. I don't know" and Hedy was
getting more and more upset...

IVO: What did Lily say?

MIA: She still had faith in Gordon, which didn't really
surprise me. I mean, that's how she is. She said she'd
talk to Hedy.

IVO: Did she?

MIA: *(Nodding)* When she walked her to school.

IVO: Before they left for the ferry?

MIA: Yes.

IVO: Do you know what she said to her?

MIA: Not for sure. But I know she wanted to tell Hedy that there are answers for her.

IVO: Of course.

MIA: Even if they're not ours, you know?

IVO: How do you mean?

MIA: I mean, that even if they're ones she finds on her own, I guess. But that there *are* answers.

IVO: I see... But there wasn't anything unusual in your conversation?

MIA: No. Just that she seemed better and I was glad. She was smiling a little, you know?

IVO: *(Nodding sympathetically)* O K. Anything else?

MIA: *(Overcome with emotion, gesturing to the bathroom)* Is it alright if I—

(IVO nods and MIA exits quickly to the bathroom. IVO follows her with his eyes for a minute.)

IVO: Mrs Ing?

RUTH: Please, call me, Ruth.

IVO: Ruth.

(In the bathroom, MIA allows herself a moment to fall apart, then quickly pulls herself together, saying "No, it's O K. It is O K" to herself like a mantra.)

RUTH: I wanted to thank you again for getting us the message from Dean and Rohm.

IVO: I was glad to do it.

RUTH: And you've been such a comfort to Mia.

IVO: Well, I think you all know I love her very much. *(After a moment)* I know this is tough on all of you.

RUTH: Ivo, my daughter Lily was a lovely person. I was proud of her. I miss her. She moved ahead too soon.

Whatever reasons there may be for that, it does not serve us to focus on them. We need to think about what is before us now. And Hedy.

IVO: Of course.

(HEDY *enters, running through the trees. She runs past* GORDON, *through the front door, past* RUTH *and into the unseen part of the house.*)

RUTH: Hedy? Hedy, honey!?

(MRS HENRI *and* GORDON *enter the house. Hearing the commotion,* MIA *comes out of the bathroom.*)

MRS HENRI: I'm sorry. Are we too soon? Hedy wasn't feeling well—

GORDON: What's wrong—?

MRS HENRI: We drove by the saw men. They've started to clear the other side and the trees were falling. She started screaming to come home.

GORDON: *(To* IVO*)* Is that all?

IVO: Yes, I think so. If there is anything else we'll—

(GORDON *goes after* HEDY.*)*

IVO: Well, I should get back. I appreciate your time. And, again, I'm sorry for your loss. Lily was very special.

RUTH: Thank you.

MIA: I'll walk you out.

(MIA *and* IVO *cross into the trees.*)

RUTH: Ida, you're welcome to stay.

MRS HENRI: Thank you but I think I'll be heading back. I'm sorry about Hedy.

RUTH: Thank you for looking after her.

(MRS HENRI *exits past* MIA *and* IVO *outside.*
ALEEAH *crosses in to* RUTH.)

ALEEAH: I hope I didn't say anything wrong Mrs.

RUTH: You told the truth.

ALEEAH: Is that what I should have done?

RUTH: Honestly, I don't know. (*She slips her monitor remote out of her waistband and looks at it.*)

ALEEAH: How are you doing?

(*Off of* RUTH's *shurg*)

ALEEAH: Should I start something for dinner?

RUTH: I suppose so. (*She goes into the rest-room where she sits, breathing.*)

(*Outside* IVO *and* MIA *walk among the trees.* IVO *looks towards the house. He sees no one looking at them.*)

IVO: I'm so sorry.

(MIA *nods.* IVO *leans in and sweetly kisses her.* MIA *breaks away.*)

MIA: I can't. I'm too upset.

IVO: Of course, I'm sorry. I'm a jerk. You're just so pretty, I can't help it.

MIA: You know Lily wouldn't go to that awful place. You know she wouldn't.

IVO: I shouldn't really talk about it with you.

MIA: I'm sure it was Gordon that convinced her to get on the ferry...

IVO: So, you think Gordon is guilty?

MIA: I'm not saying that. I just... Anyway, they never saw Doctor Uda so it doesn't matter.

IVO: Intent is a crime, honey. It's less severe, but it's still a crime.

MIA: So, what would happen? Would he got to prison or something?

IVO: If he's guilty. The law is the law and if he broke it, no matter how sad his situation is, he has to pay for it.

MIA: But what would happen to Hedy?

IVO: She has you and your Mom and, from what you said, it seems like it might be better for Hedy if he wasn't around—

MIA: It's just his ideas—or lack of them, I guess— that bother me. That's all I'm saying.

IVO: I understand. But, we shouldn't talk about it anymore.

MIA: O K. *(After a moment)* You could probably tell, but Aleeah's thinking of not staying on.

IVO: She can't wait a while?

MIA: She wants to get on with her own life, I guess.

IVO: How's Hedy taking it?

MIA: She doesn't know yet.

IVO: Well, it's for the best, her going.

MIA: I don't know who bothers me more, Gordon or Aleeah. *(After a moment, looking to the area of rescue)* When will the Area be done?

IVO: Next couple of weeks.

MIA: Are they going to do drills or something? Show us what to do?

IVO: After most of them are finished, there's a two-part special about how the whole thing works. They'll show that and then someone will come out and demonstrate.

MIA: Do you think it'll work?

IVO: It'll do what it's supposed to do.

MIA: *(Responding to his tone)* But...?

IVO: I just wished they could've done something bigger.

MIA: I thought you said they're building millions of them.

IVO: Yeah, but it's all about *dealing* with the problem. I wanted them to try *solving* the problem.

MIA: Well, it's complicated, right? Sometimes there isn't an answer when things get too complicated.

IVO: I thought you said there always was an answer.

MIA: *(She points to her heart)* To *these* things... *(She points to the Area of Rescue)* Not to *those* things.

IVO: Well, I've got to get back. I've got Friday night free. Let's go somewhere.

MIA: O K.

IVO: How about The Circle?

MIA: Really?!

IVO: Why not?

MIA: You could get us in?

IVO: You underestimate how important I am.

(She smiles. He kisses her and starts to walks off.)

IVO: Oh, next week, my parents are having an anniversary party. You're invited.

MIA: That's nice.

IVO: Thirty years.

MIA: Wow. They were young, huh?

IVO: Same age we are.

MIA: Is that a hint?

IVO: I'm just saying.

MIA: *(Smiling)* O K.

(Inside, HEDY *frantically runs into the living room, turns on the film of the man playing violin. She takes up her violin and follows along.* GORDON *follows her out.)*

GORDON: *(Continuing a conversation)* Hedy, honey. I'm sorry. There is nothing I can do about your trees. We'll sit and have dinner and you'll feel better.

HEDY: Stop saying that! I won't feel better.

GORDON: I know you can't imagine it now, but—

HEDY: I'll stop telling you how I feel so you can think I feel better, but I won't. *Ever.*

GORDON: You will, honey. I know it's hard now, but—

HEDY: Leave me alone!

GORDON: I'm just trying to help.

HEDY: Your help doesn't help. Your help is to help *you* not to help me.

GORDON: Hedy!

*(*RUTH *goes to* GORDON *and pulls him away. All lights go to black except the video/film of the older man playing the violin.)*

(Transition)

(The trees are cut. They fall. Only stumps remain.)

Scene 3

(Twilight. Outside, the trees are now stumps.)

*(*HEDY *stands before the film playing quietly.* RUTH *approaches her.* HEDY *plays slower and slower until she comes to a stop.* RUTH *takes the violin out of her hands. As she does,* HEDY *suddenly hugs her very tightly. Then, just as suddenly, she lets go and leans against the back wall, the image of the man playing over her.* RUTH *mutes the sound.)*

HEDY: Why did Papa make this?

RUTH: He made it for you.

HEDY: But he didn't know I'd like to play.

RUTH: He made a good guess.

HEDY: How did he know I'd like it?

RUTH: He thought you'd be like him, and your mother.

HEDY: But she played that other thing you used to have.

RUTH: The piano. But she was musical, like you.

HEDY: There's a girl at school, she plays the violin, too.

RUTH: Really?

HEDY: She was surprised that I did since only the really, really rich kids play instruments. Most of them haven't ever seen a violin.

RUTH: I guess there are more important things.

HEDY: Not to me.

(There is a knock at the door. RUTH *turns the film off.* MRS HENRI *stands at the door with a container.)*

RUTH: It's Mrs Henri. Do you want to play outside for a minute?

HEDY: In the stump-yard?! It's repulsive.

RUTH: So, you'd rather stay and talk with Mrs Henri?

(HEDY *goes to the door and opens it.*)

MRS HENRI: Well, hello, dear.

(HEDY *nods and lets* MRS HENRI *in but passes by her, going out to the trees.*)

RUTH: Hello, Ida.

MRS HENRI: I've just brought over a little bit of casserole. Ed and his wife were supposed to make it over with the boys, but there was a blockade on the highway and they had to turn around.

RUTH: That's a shame.

MRS HENRI: Anyway, I put a bunch in the freezer, but I thought I'd bring some over, save you the trouble of dinner.

(RUTH *takes the casserole and walks towards the kitchen.* HEDY *wanders out of sight.*)

RUTH: That was thoughtful. Thank you. Can I get you anything?

MRS HENRI: Oh, no, I'll only stay a minute.

(MRS HENRI *sits down.* RUTH *brings them both a glass of water.*)

RUTH: Well, sit down. Make yourself comfortable.

MRS HENRI: Where's your girl?

RUTH: Aleeah has the afternoon off.

MRS HENRI: That's nice of you.

RUTH: Oh, it's in the contract—two afternoons a week.

MRS HENRI: Really? Ed's wife Duri has a girl and I thought she only had off every other Saturday or something. Not that they work her very hard. *(Taking*

the water from RUTH*)* Thank you. *(Taking a sip of water)*
Your water always tastes better than mine. I know I've
asked you and I've tried what you use, but mine just
doesn't taste as good, I swear.

RUTH: I wish I had the secret.

MRS HENRI: *(Changing the subject)* You know, Ruth,
we widows must lean on each other. No one else cares
for us. You know I am here for you in this life and in
the time ahead.

RUTH: That's kind of you to say.

MRS HENRI: Of course, I am. I was certain you knew
that. Which is why I was just a little hurt to hear from
Mia about Lily.

RUTH: Well, as you know, something like that is so
overwhelming. I did try to tell everyone myself, but
I didn't have the strength.

MRS HENRI: Oh, no, dear, not about the accident.
About Lily being pregnant.

RUTH: Well...how did that ever come up?

MRS HENRI: Well, I was saying to Mia how difficult it's
been for you these last few years without your boys
around you. And she mentioned the double tragedy
of both Lily and the baby being lost in the accident.

RUTH: Oh. I see.

MRS HENRI: I was so sorry you didn't feel like you
could share your burden with me.

RUTH: *(Very lightly)* Well, Ida, you always seem plenty
burdened.

MRS HENRI: But I'm not, truly. Not for a friend like you.
(After a moment) I happened to mention the baby to
Duri, you know Ed's wife... *(Gently)* Who is expecting
their third.

RUTH: Yes, congratulations.

(GORDON *appears in the trees and speaks with* HEDY *for a bit.*)

MRS HENRI: Well, Duri happened to mention to Doctor Edvan about Lily's tragedy and they had a bit of a misunderstanding, because Doctor Edvan seemed to be saying that Lily's baby had already been lost... before the accident.

RUTH: Yes. Just before the accident, they found out the baby had moved ahead. They had a birthing appointment scheduled for a few days after the accident.

MRS HENRI: *(Understanding)* Oh, I see. I see. At least she was spared all the pain of that.

(GORDON *walks through the door. He immediately takes off his I D badge.*)

GORDON: *(Seeing* MRS HENRI*)* Hello.

MRS HENRI: Hello, Gordon. *(Standing)* Well...I imagine you all will be getting on to dinner, so I'll make my way home.

RUTH: Ida and I were just speaking about Lily's pregnancy and your loss.

GORDON: *(After a moment)* Oh.

RUTH: Duri, Ed's wife, heard about it from Doctor Edvan.

GORDON: I see.

MRS HENRI: I didn't mean to bring up anything upsetting...I just... Again, I am so sorry for your loss. I hope you know we are shoulders to lean on. *(Almost at the door)* Enjoy that casserole.

GORDON: What did you come for, Mrs. Henri?

RUTH: Gordon, I think we've said what we have to say.

GORDON: No, go ahead. Really. Please.

MRS HENRI: Well, I did want to tell you something—something that I think no one else would be brave enough to tell you—because it is unpleasant in the extreme. Now, I don't believe it for a second, but you should know what is being said, because what is being said can have as bad an effect as if it were true.

GORDON: Well, what is it?

MRS HENRI: You should know, Gordon, that people are saying that you and Lily were going to see Doctor Uda.

RUTH: Well, Ida, you know as well as we do that people will talk. There is nothing much we can do about it.

GORDON: *(Cracking a little)* What if it's true?

RUTH: Gordon....

GORDON: No, what if it is true? What if the grief was too much? What if Lily had to have it finished and this was the only way? Would it really be a crime?

MRS HENRI: Well...yes. You know it is a crime.

GORDON: Even if the baby isn't alive?

MRS HENRI: The law does not specify. Gordon, yours was the worst case scenario. The laws are not made for the worst case scenario. The law can't accommodate like that. So, although I'm sorry for it, it was not the right thing to do. But, you didn't make it, so I guess there is comfort in that.

GORDON: *(Stunned)* Is there?

MRS HENRI: I just mean...I just mean it would have been horrible if on top of the accident, if...well, I'm sorry for it. But you should be careful. You are an upstanding member of the community. What kind of message does this send out to the children?

GORDON: What kind of message...?

MRS HENRI: I know it is some kind of test of our strength that keeps the specter of evil in our midst, the shimmer of that red house across the water. But it is one thing to have degenerate people who commit awful crimes because they are detached from their better nature—we can only reflect and hope they find their way back—and it is *another* thing to have people like you and Lily, respectable, faces of the faith supporting such atrocities. Think of Hedy. *(After a moment)* Well, I think you have had enough sadness. I certainly won't think to cause you any more. *(Pausing at the door)* But I would be on the lookout if I were you. Mia's been awfully free with that young service man and another trip to Doctor Uda this family could not well afford.

GORDON: Is that a threat? Is that a *threat*?

(GORDON steps in and blocks the door from MRS HENRI.)

MRS HENRI: Ruth, he's frightening me.

GORDON: *(Stepping in on her)* You should be careful who you condemn.

MRS HENRI: Please permit me to go.

(A beeping sound is heard. RUTH takes the monitor out of her waistband.)

GORDON: Ruth—?

RUTH: *(Very short of breath)* I just need a minute.

MRS HENRI: Ruth—?

(RUTH goes into the bathroom. She sits, breathes, and listens at the door.)

MRS HENRI: *(Stepping back, trying to smile)* Gordon, I understand you are beside yourself with grief. I understand. I do. When I lost my Josephine, I never thought I'd be able to feel happiness—

GORDON: I saw Edward not too long ago. *(After a moment)* Downtown.

MRS HENRI: Oh, well, Edward often has meetings. Downtown.

GORDON: I saw him go into a restaurant. I don't know what it was called because there's no sign on the door. I looked in and saw him there with a man I went to University with—Ian Watzman. Have you ever met Mister Watzman, Mrs Henri?

MRS HENRI: I'm not sure. Edward has so many business acquaintances.

GORDON: Yes, I'm sure he does. But the thing I found strange is that Ian doesn't really work. He comes from a very wealthy family. And I wasn't sure why someone of Ian's stature would be meeting with Edward, or anyone in waste engineering for that matter, as well liked as Edward is...

MRS HENRI: Oh, Ian Watzman. Yes. I remember now. Edward and Ian met during their service years. And, perhaps, they are still in touch. You know, service often makes a lasting bond between men.

GORDON: Yes, I suppose that's true. But, I didn't think Ian finished his service years. His father bought him out, I think. Which didn't surprise me.

MRS HENRI: Oh.

GORDON: You see...rumors were always following him. He was what some people considered...odd.

MRS HENRI: Well, I don't think he and Edward have any sort of regular contact. I wouldn't be surprised if they had just run in to each other by accident and—

GORDON: You know, I thought the same thing. But, since I was there, I thought I'd stick around and say hello to Edward. So, I waited. I saw them leave the

restaurant and walk around the side, away from the
security camera. They walked into the alley, behind a
removal bin. But, from where I was standing, I could
still see them, Mrs Henri. I could see them put their
arms around each other—

MRS HENRI: Well, if Ian is as wealthy as you say, I am
sure he has spent some time in Europe. And men do
say goodbye differently there than they do here and—

GORDON: I *saw* them, Mrs Henri. I took a clip of them.

MRS HENRI: Everyone knows better then to take a clip
at face value anymore.

GORDON: Don't you know what people say about
Edward, Mrs Henri? Have always said about Edward?

MRS HENRI: Edward has a beautiful wife and is about
to have his third child—

GORDON: But you should *know* what is being said—

MRS HENRI: If people are jealous and saying silly
things—

GORDON: Because what is being said—

MRS HENRI: It doesn't mean—

GORDON: Can have as bad an effect as if it were true!

MRS HENRI: *(Snapping)* But it's *not* true!!

GORDON: My wife and I were on the ferry going to the
children's hospital. The weather was rough and my
wife slipped and fell and drowned. That's all. That is
the story you will tell, that you will correct people on
when they get it wrong. Just like I will say Edward and
Geddeth are just old service friends who occasionally
bump into each other and have lunch.

MRS HENRI: *(After a long moment)* Yes. Of course.

GORDON: *(Opening the door)* Go home.

MRS HENRI: Gordon, I...I didn't mean....

GORDON: Never come here again.

(She goes. RUTH *emerges. She and* GORDON *have a long look.)*

RUTH: I don't know how this will go now.

GORDON: Neither do I. I'm sorry. *(He slowly sinks to sitting.)* Why did Lily listen to Aleeah? Such a crazy story!

RUTH: Aleeah's story?

GORDON: *(Almost to himself)* Lily was always so sure of everything...why did that story shake her up? *(To* RUTH*)* Did you know? Did you know she couldn't get it out of her head?

RUTH: What Lily was thinking and feeling has no bearing on what happened—

GORDON: She said she could hear the baby crying, that she was the only one who knew him, so no one else could go to him— *(Unraveling)* As long as she was here, she said, he would be alone, crying in the dark and she couldn't—

RUTH: *(Trying to comfort and calm)* It's alright.

GORDON: I should have known!

RUTH: Gordon look at me.

GORDON: *(Confessing)* She begged me to take her out on the ferry. She begged me. She said she couldn't wait another second, it had to be finished. When the ferry wasn't going to go, she put the money in my hand to pay the ferryman. But I should have known she never, *never* would have gone there. I should have known!

RUTH: It was an accident. It was an accident.

GORDON: She didn't slip, Ruth.

RUTH: *(Trying desperately to keep him from saying the words)* No. Gordon, please. *Please—*

GORDON: She jumped. *(After a moment)* She kissed my hand and said we both had a child to take care of— one in this world and one in the next. The boat lurched and...she jumped.

(Transition)

(Perhaps the sky is filled with hundreds of dying, shooting stars.)

Scene 4

(It is night. MIA and IVO walk towards the house. They linger, kissing in the trees. They are laughing and smiling.)

IVO: You promise you mean it.

MIA: Of course!

IVO: You just looked so surprised.

MIA: I was surprised.

IVO: I've been hinting forever and I thought you were...

MIA: I am. I *am.* I was just surprised. *(She looks to the ring on her finger.)*

IVO: You want me to come in and tell your Mom with you?

MIA: No. It's too late. I'm sure she's asleep. We can tell them all at Aleeah's party.

IVO: Great.

(They kiss.)

MIA: I should....

IVO: Yeah.

(They kiss again. MIA makes her way to the door.)

IVO: Mia...?

MIA: Yeah?

IVO: One last thing.

MIA: What?

IVO: I wanted to tell you, but there didn't seem to be a right time...

MIA: *(Stricken, afraid)* What? You're making me—

IVO: No, it's not—

MIA: Is it Dean or Rohm? Are they O K?

IVO: No, they're fine, as far as I know. No, it's Gordon.

MIA: Yeah?

IVO: They are going to press charges.

MIA: What kind of charges?

IVO: Intent, like I told you.

MIA: No. No! They can't. What about Hedy?

(Inside the house, RUTH, dressed in night clothes, comes out and stands near the door, listening.)

IVO: It doesn't mean he'll get convicted. But, they feel there was enough evidence...

MIA: Who felt? You did the interviews? I mean—Ivo!?! What did you tell them!

IVO: It was clear from what you said that Gordon—

MIA: From what I said? I didn't mean— You're not doing this for *me*?

IVO: I thought this is what you wanted. You were very clear that Gordon is pretty morally bankrupt and—

MIA: I didn't—! How could you think it was what I wanted?

IVO: Didn't you?

MIA: No! I mean, maybe in the abstract or whatever, but not to have him taken away or...how could you think that?

IVO: I'm sorry, I thought—

MIA: Is there anything that you can do? Anything?

IVO: I don't think so. I mean, the wheels are turning. It doesn't mean he'll get convicted.

MIA: There's *nothing* you can do? Please, honey— there must be something...?

IVO: I don't know...

MIA: Please...please...for Hedy. For me.

IVO: I'll talk to my supervisor. But, I'm not sure—

MIA: *(Nodding)* O K. O K.

IVO: I'm sorry, I thought this was what you wanted—

MIA: Just talk to them. Talk to them, O K?

(IVO nods. MIA steps away. RUTH steps away from the door, moving towards the unseen part of the house.)

IVO: Hey, come here.

(He goes to MIA and puts his arms around her, but the energy between them is totally changed.)

IVO: I feel like I just ruined the best night of my life.

MIA: No, I did.

(MIA goes into the house. IVO goes. MIA leans her head against the door, looking at her engagement ring. RUTH steps forward.)

RUTH: Hi.

(MIA hides her hand.)

MIA: Did you hear any of that?

RUTH: Some.

MIA: About Gordon?

(Off RUTH's *nod)*

MIA: It's my fault. What I said.

*(*MIA *falls into* RUTH's *arms.* RUTH *holds* MIA *for a moment.)*

RUTH: You have something else you want to tell me?

MIA: Not at the moment.

*(*RUTH *takes* MIA's *hand.)*

RUTH: You two are awfully young.

MIA: I want to be settled, Mom. We believe the same things. We want the same things. I just want to be settled and safe and...

RUTH: Do you love him?

MIA: What does that mean, really? I think I do.

RUTH: Does he make you... *(Fanning herself)* You know...

MIA: Are we really talking about this?

RUTH: It's important.

MIA: That is not the only thing, you know.

RUTH: But it's part of it.

MIA: I understand how this would work with Ivo. It makes sense.

RUTH: That's not the best reason.

MIA: It is to me. But how could he think that I wanted...?

RUTH: Because you don't approve of Gordon.

MIA: I don't *agree* with him. But that doesn't mean I want him taken away or something.

RUTH: You don't think Hedy would be better off without him?

MIA: No. I mean, not in a *practical* sense.

RUTH: Then in what sense?

MIA: I don't know. But I didn't want *this*. I'll do everything I can to make this better, I will. For Hedy.

RUTH: I know. *(After a moment)* We should get some sleep. *(She begins to go.)*

MIA: Mom...

RUTH: Yes...?

MIA: You...you don't believe anymore, do you? Not really. Not like you used to.

RUTH: I do...but it's different. It's not in a way I think anyone else could understand.

MIA: Oh.

RUTH: Does that make you sad?

MIA: Yeah, it does.

RUTH: It happens sometimes when you live a long life. You'll see.

(RUTH goes. MIA crosses back outside. She looks at the Area of Rescue.)

MIA: Maybe.

(Transition)

(Night becomes day—perhaps there is a terrible downpour during which ALEEAH sings a song in her native language)

Scene 5

(The next afternoon. HEDY *wanders in between the stumps outside.* GORDON *and* ALEEAH, *who wears an I D badge that looks like* GORDON's, *walks up to* HEDY. *They talk with her for a moment.* GORDON *and* ALEEAH *then go to the house where* RUTH, MIA *and* IVO *are waiting.* HEDY *follows.)*

RUTH: *(To* ALEEAH*)* You got it?

*(*ALEEAH *holds out her new I D badge.)*

ALEEAH: I got it.

RUTH: Congratulations!

MIA: Congratulation!

RUTH: Sit down. I made a cake. We'll have some.

MIA: Well, now that everyone's here, we have some good news, too.

RUTH: What's that?

MIA: The investigation is concluded.

RUTH: It is?

MIA: It is.

IVO: It was judged an accident. The case is closed.

RUTH: *(Very evenly)* As it should be. Now we can all be at peace about it.

ALEEAH: I knew everything would be alright! *(Closing her eyes)* I can feel them—Mister Ing, Lily and the little one—

GORDON: *(Weakly)* Aleeah, please...

ALEEAH: Oh, Gordon, don't be sad—they are all so happy knowing that everything has come out all right! They are—

RUTH: Aleeah, please. It's enough.

ALEEAH: *(Very sincerely)* I just want you to know—everything is alright now.

MIA: And we have one other bit of news. Mom, already knows but... *(She holds out her hand with an engagement ring on her finger.)*

ALEEAH: Oh, Mia, congratulations!

HEDY: What?

GORDON: Your Aunt is getting married.

HEDY: To who? Not to Ivo?!

MIA: Yes, to Ivo!

HEDY: Why?!

RUTH: We've too much to celebrate. Come, we'll go out to dinner. We'll go somewhere.

HEDY: *(Leaning against the wall)* I'm not celebrating anything.

ALEEAH: *(To HEDY)* Come on, celebrate with us!

GORDON: You all should go. I'll stay with Hedy.

(ALEEAH goes to HEDY and talks to her by the wall.)

RUTH: *(To MIA)* Come here. Let me see that ring again.

(RUTH takes MIA away from GORDON and IVO.)

GORDON: *(To IVO)* I hope you'll be happy. I feel almost like a second father to Mia. I've been in the family since she was younger than Hedy.

IVO: I guess I should've asked you for her hand or whatever. I didn't think about it.

GORDON: No, of course.

(GORDON and IVO continue to talk quietly as RUTH and MIA's conversation becomes audible.)

RUTH: You're sure?

MIA: You have no idea what he did to get this fixed.

RUTH: You can still change your mind.

MIA: It's O K. It'll be good. It'll be fine.

GORDON: *(To IVO)* Well, I hope you'll be happy. And thank you.

IVO: It wasn't too easy getting the thing squared away. But, seeing how we're about to be family....

GORDON: Well, congratulations.

IVO: But, even being family, I'd have to pursue something in the future, should anything unusual come up.

(GORDON nods.)

MIA: Where should we go to eat? Mom, please make Hedy come.

HEDY: I'm *not* going.

IVO: Come on, Kiddo! I'm going to be your Uncle! That's something to celebrate, isn't it?

(HEDY takes the pin IVO gave her, throws it to the floor and elaborately stomps on it.)

MIA: Hedy! Gordon! Stop her!

GORDON: Hedy! Stop! Hedy!

(HEDY stops and leans again the wall staring at IVO.)

MIA: I don't know what's gotten into her. Ivo, I'm sorry, I—

IVO: It's alright. *(He picks up the pin.)*

RUTH: You three go. We'll meet you in a bit. Let us come back to our senses and we'll meet you. How about steak?

MIA: No! Really?!

RUTH: It's a special occasion. Go. We'll be right there.

(IVO *and* MIA *pass by* GORDON *and* HEDY.)

IVO: (*To* HEDY) I know you are having a hard time of it, Hedder. Don't worry.

(IVO *hands the pin to* GORDON *with a look.* ALEEAH *follows them out.* GORDON *grabs* HEDY *by the arms, holding her very tightly.*)

GORDON: You need to listen to me. You need to listen to me very closely. I understand that you're mad. I know that you don't like Ivo because he is connected to the people who took away your trees. But you need to listen to me. You can never, never, never talk to Ivo that way again, or treat him that way again. Do you understand me? He is connected to people that can make a lot of trouble for us and we need to stay clear of that so we can stay safe, O K? So that we can be safe.

HEDY: You said I should say what I think. You said there were no bad questions.

GORDON: I know. I know.

HEDY: Isn't he supposed to protect *us*? Why am I scared of him if he's supposed to protect *us*?

GORDON: It's just the way it is!

HEDY: (*After a moment*) Where is she?

GORDON: Who, honey?

HEDY: Mama.

GORDON: She's gone. You know that.

HEDY: She said she'd always be with me, but I don't know where she is, I can't see her.

GORDON: I don't know what to tell you... *(Realizing he has to tell her something)* It's not something you can see. It's something you feel.

HEDY: *(A confession)* But...I don't feel anything.

GORDON: I know, honey.

HEDY: I don't feel anything.

(GORDON hugs HEDY. GORDON and RUTH look at each other a moment.)

HEDY: Do we have to stay here? Now that the trees are gone, do we have to stay here?

GORDON: I don't know where there is for us to go.

HEDY: I don't want to stay. Please, Daddy, don't make us stay.

GORDON: Why don't you go outside, honey? We'll be right there.

(HEDY grabs her bluebird and exits to the tree stumps.)

RUTH: It was close, Gordon. You have to be careful.

GORDON: It's over. What can they do to me now?

RUTH: Maybe you should go away for a while. It would be good for Hedy, a change of scenery. My sister has that place, you know, by the water. For the summer...

GORDON: So, go hide out? Is that what I'm supposed to do now, go hide out like...?

RUTH: Just for the summer.

GORDON: When did this happen? It didn't use to be like this...

RUTH: It did. And then it didn't. And now it is again...

GORDON: But only for the summer. I can't be run out. I won't be run out.

RUTH: Just for the summer.

(Lights go to black except for a light on HEDY *standing on a tree stump.)*

(Transition)

(Slowly, ash starts to fall.)

Scene 6

*(*HEDY *still stands on a stump, the ash falling from the sky all around her.)*

(In the living room, GORDON, RUTH, *and* MIA, IVO *talk with* ALEEAH *who stands by the door.)*

GORDON: *(To* ALEEAH*)* Thanks for coming. I know it meant a lot to Hedy.

ALEEAH: Of course. Good to see you all. This will probably be the last visit for a long time. I'm moving to the Rey-haul district.

RUTH: You are?

ALEEAH: *(Nodding)* It's easier to be with people from home. They know where you come from.

IVO: I think that's true.

RUTH: Well, let us know how to reach you when you get settled.

ALEEAH: I will. *(To* IVO *and* MIA*)* Congratulations again on your wedding.

IVO: Thank you.

*(*MIA *nods.* ALEEAH *walks out among the trees to* HEDY.*)*

ALEEAH: *(Looking at the ash)* They're getting close now. *(To* HEDY) I'll miss you.

HEDY: You could come.

ALEEAH: I'm sorry, honey, I can't. You know. But you're going to do fine there.

HEDY: It's just for the summer.

ALEEAH: Of course.

(ALEEAH and HEDY hug. HEDY watches ALEEAH go. Back in the house, GORDON has finished saying goodbye to MIA, IVO and RUTH.)

RUTH: Let us know when you get there.

GORDON: I will. *(He walks outside, carrying the violin case. To HEDY.)* You said your goodbyes?

HEDY: Yes.

(RUTH calls to HEDY through the window.)

RUTH: Hedy!

(HEDY runs to the window. RUTH presses her hand against the glass. HEDY does the same. After a moment, GORDON hands the violin case to HEDY.)

HEDY: You have Papa's lessons?

GORDON: Of course, we wouldn't leave Papa.

(Inside, RUTH turns to MIA and IVO. She puts her hand on MIA's cheek in a loving gesture.)

RUTH: Excuse me.

IVO: Of course.

(RUTH goes to the bathroom where she sits and breathes, looking at her heart monitor.)

(Outside, HEDY hands GORDON back the violin case.)

HEDY: Can you carry this for a minute? I'll be right there.

(HEDY *watches* GORDON *go, then takes the bluebird from her pocket.* MIA *looks out the window at* HEDY.)

MIA: *(Very conflicted)* I'm sad to see them go. But, it's just for the summer.

IVO: Of course.

(*They walk to the unseen part of the house. Outside,* HEDY *kisses the bluebird, puts it on a stump and looks above.*)

HEDY: It's for you. (*Waiting to feel something*) Nothing. (*She buries the bird in a pile of ash and walks away. She stops, gets the bird, shakes it off, puts it on the stump. To the bird*) Good-bye.

(*She stands for a moment looking at it, ash raining down hard. She exits. Light fade to only the bluebird getting covered in ash.*)

END OF PLAY

www.ingramcontent.com/pod-product-compliance
Lightning Source LLC
Chambersburg PA
CBHW052220090426

42741CB00010B/2615